Raising Money

Insights for startups and small business –

from a master entrepreneur

Dave Berkus

Published by David Berkus, DBA The Berkus Press.

For corrections, company/title updates, comments, or any other inquiries, please e-mail DBerkus@berkus.com

Second Printing 2014
10 9 8 7 6 5 4 3 2

ISBN: 978-1-105-04065-8

The content within this book has been previously published within the books, BERKONOMICS, and ADVANCED BERKONOMICS. Individual insights from this book are published periodically in Dave's emails and blog, www.berkonomics.com.

Groups may order copies of the book at a group discount by contacting Dave Berkus at 626-355-5375, or at dberkus@berkus.com .

Throughout this book, the Cambria type font was used for headlines, and text was set using the Calibri font.

The views expressed by the individuals in this book do not necessarily reflect the views shared by the companies they are employed by (or the companies mentioned in) this book. The employment status and affiliations of author with the companies referenced are subject to change.

INTRODUCTION

This book is the second in a series of eight short, easy to read books that guide an entrepreneur through the stages of creation, management, growth, and ultimately sale of a small business enterprise. And this is the second edition of this book, packed with half again as much materials the first edition, published in 2011.

Each section is an insight into another facet of starting a business that is not taught in business school or available in business texts, but rather the result of over fifty years of entrepreneurial experience with my own entrepreneurial companies and serving as investor, coach, mentor and board member for over forty entrepreneurial startups over the years.

Originally published as portions of three books, BASIC BERKONOMICS, BERKONOMCS, and ADVANCED BERKONOMICS, comments from entrepreneurs and professional managers after reading those books led to suggestions that I create separate mini-books for each stage of the business, to appeal to the interests of those at that stage of development, ready to absorb and implement insights that apply directly to the current stage of their business. Make them inexpensive and available as eBooks, they suggested, so that entire teams of managers could use the book as a planning tool and discussion prompt for the team in meetings.

And so this series of Small Business Success Books was born to address an opportunity. You can pick up this book and immediately relate to the insights, issues, opportunities, and exercises in this book right at the earliest stages of creating your business. This is not a replacement for "how to" books, courses, and consultants. It is a deeper opportunity to evaluate, plan, and execute strategies for growth based upon these insights that augment and amplify the usual "how to" materials available to entrepreneurs.

In this book, I'll tell personal stories from my fifty-plus years of entrepreneurial experience. But every one of us has a story to add to this mix, one of passionate entrepreneurism, sometimes inside an existing larger corporation, sometimes alone on a kitchen table, or back room desk. And it is a sure thing that many of us will have cogent, insightful additions to this caldron, culled from their own experiences. There's a place for these in the blog, www.berkonomics.com, and I welcome any and all for others to read and learn.

Dave Berkus

Arcadia, California

P.S. This is the sixteenth publication from *The Berkus Press*. I am very fortunate to have expert help this time from some very smart friends in the business, each of whom has volunteered to contribute one or more insights for this book, directly from their personal experience of working as an entrepreneur or with entrepreneurs. Here's a special thanks to these friends, whose contributions are definitely for your benefit. Whenever one of these excellent insights appear in this book, the first time each contributor's work appears, I'll insert a very short bio for that expert right below the headline. And as always, if no attribution appears for an insight, I'm its author - and to be blamed for any and all errors in judgment and accuracy.

Contents

Raising Money

This stage is critical to many businesses and a passing option to others, depending upon the capital efficiency of the enterprise. Some businesses require very little capital and the founder is able to self-finance the enterprise and retain 100% of its ownership and control from ignition through liquidity event (startup through sale). For you who fit that description, nice work. For the rest of us desiring to build large, valuable enterprises quickly, the need for outside capital is high on our list of requirements and even the source for some sleepless nights as we worry over the availability and cost of capital. It is for this group that we explore the implications implicit in raising money for growth.

Before we explore the first insight, it might be useful to list some of the ways in which you can raise money for growth with and without outside investors.

Bootstrapping: This term describes your ability to start a business with little investment and grow it using internally-generated funds. Certainly bootstrapping is a preferred method of funding growth if it does not hold back the speed of growth or hobble the quality of product or service to the extent that better-funded competitors can overtake the business. There is a lot to say about retaining control. You will realize much more from the ultimate sale of your business even if at a considerably lower price than if splitting the proceeds with investors. You will have more control over strategy and execution than with an outside board overseeing planning and performance. But few businesses grow into the sweet spot of $20 million to $30 million in worth to an ultimate buyer without the injection of outside capital.

Friends, family and fools: This term, although pejorative, describes the typical mix of early investors in a small, young growing business. Money from these sources is relatively easy to come by, and most often comes with no strings as to oversight by a formal board composed of these investors and management. However, most often, these funds are solicited by a well-meaning entrepreneur from investors who are not qualified as accredited investors under the law (currently requiring a proved income of $200,000 a year or $1 million in net worth for an individual investor). I've arrived at a significant number of companies that were looking for additional growth capital after a "friends and family" round, and had to "clean up" the cap table more than a few times over the years. Taking this kind of money has a number of pitfalls you should be aware of. It is most common to greatly overprice such a round of financing, valuing the enterprise well above what it may be worth at the moment for friend or related investors who do not have the sophistication or willingness to challenge the valuation. When professional investors look at such overvalued prior investments, they may refuse to become involved with a company, knowing that there will be, at the very least, universal disappointment and anger from prior investors when a new round is priced lower than the earlier friends and family round. Sometimes this money is just too available and the risks seem so far away; so an entrepreneur will take the money and put off the worry over the eventual consequences, all in the hope that no more investment will ever be needed and everyone will be richer for the effort.

Using your bank credit line and credit cards: Even with the credit crunch signaled by the recent recession, many banks will issue business credit cards with a $50,000 limit if the entrepreneur is willing to personally guarantee the balance, and has the net worth to do so. And even with the significant cost of credit card debt, many entrepreneurs aggressively use existing cards to finance a startup. It's an option, even though an expensive one.

"Strategic partner" investors: If you can find a strategic partner willing to invest in your enterprise, consider it a blessing. Whether the partner is a supplier looking to gain a lock on your business as it grows or a customer looking to create a competitive barrier through use of your product, such an investment typically carries fewer restrictions than from a professional investor and less oversight. Better yet, the valuation of your enterprise is often higher than if the same investment were taken from a professional investor. Strategic investors validate a business, by their presence creating the very value they pay for with increased price per share purchased. It is most often a win-win for both you and the strategic partner.

Professional angels: This is the arena where I work and play. This class of investor, once quite disorganized, has become much like the venture capital community, creating a process including due diligence (careful examination of a business before investment), terms of investment that match those of venture capitalists, and a process that often takes months from introduction to investment. Yet, professional angels are usually willing to take active board seats in a young enterprise and act as cost-free consultants to the CEO-entrepreneur, giving freely of their individual and collective years of experience, often in the same industry as the investment target. Do not expect grand valuations of your enterprise from these professional angels. They have been burned too badly during the last decade by overvaluing businesses and finding themselves like friends and family, "stuffed" into a down round of lower valuation when a company takes its next round of financing from the next step, venture capitalists. Professional angels, often organized into groups, usually invest from $100,000 to $1 million in a young enterprise.

Venture, private equity and more: Here we lump a large number investor classes into one. Venture capital comes with a cost, and there are no bargains for the company when taking such an investment. VC's value an enterprise lower than others might at the same stage of investment, always aware of the need to create opportunities for "home run" profits at exit, since over fifty percent of their investments typically are lost when companies die before an opportunity to sell to others. Further, as a class, VC's have not done well for their own investors over the past decade since the bubble burst, making it doubly important to fight for low valuations and high profits at exit. VC's do not even engage in discussion with most of those entrepreneurs seeking capital. By some estimates, 95% of contacts are ignored unless they come as referrals from trusted sources such as known lawyers, accountants or fellow VC's. And just for measure, VC's fund less than 2% of all deals they do investigate. Typical VC investments begin at $2 million and quickly rise to $5 million and above, depending upon the size of the fund and stage of investment. Terms are much more restrictive than from strategic or angel investors, often requiring the entrepreneur to escrow his or her founder stock for a number of years to prevent the founder leaving, and restricting the sale of prior stock without the VC also being allowed to offer a share of its holdings in the same sale.

Private equity investments are available from firms created for this later stage opportunity, but typically are available only for businesses that have achieved revenues well above $50 million. Often private equity investors will want control of the business as well.

Bank lines of credit are often available to businesses that are profitable, most often personally guaranteed by the entrepreneur, but available at a cost in interest less than most any other source. Small Business Administration (SBA) federally-guaranteed bank loans are becoming available again after years of limited activity. With some restrictive provisions, these loans are favored by many banks as carrying much less risk than loans without the guarantee.

But it is the outside investor that validates a business, often influencing growth with shared relationships, experienced guidance and providing a gateway to needed resources. There are a few insights that relate to this money resource, and you should know and respect these...

Three things you need to have when raising money.

Here's more advice from professional investors for aspiring entrepreneurs. Each of us has a list of things we look for early on when identifying whether we want to go to the next step in analyzing a plan. Come to think of it, these are good for challenging any business plan.

First: You must address *a big market,* large enough to allow a new entrant to have a shot at making a dent with a great product or service, and growing to a size that will make the company valuable at the exit. We often draw the line at believing that a company can capture enough of the market to generate over $40 million in revenues by the fifth year in the market. Many, many businesses will never be able to obtain this kind of market size or share. And often, these are the ones that will be bypassed by most organized angel groups when considering funding. Your big market can come from having a dominant share or just by being in a very large space. Both work - with the dominant share being preferred.

Second, you must have and be able to tell *an easy to understand story* to your prospective customers, suppliers and investors. If your product is too complex to describe in a few words, your opportunity to sell it will suffer, and investors will quickly lose interest or the ability to follow your explanation. I've often repeated that entrepreneurs must construct a short, single sentence "mantra" that explains what you do in as few words as possible, sometimes using the name of a well-known company as a proxy for your activities. "We are the Skype of Internet one-to many interactive broadcasting."

And third, you must have some *"secret sauce"* that is unique, and makes you and your offering stand out among the thousands of possible competitors. What gives you a head start, a barrier to entry, an extra value that others cannot easily emulate? Secret sauce is important to investors and to you in competing against a company with more money, a brand name, or a head start.

A big market. An easy-to-understand story. Secret sauce. Why not spend a few minutes right now, and explain to yourself how you address each.

Back to basics: List the forms of capital available.

There are a number of options available to finance your startup or existing business. These options may or may not work for you depending on many factors. So we'll spend the next several cycles delving into these, helping you to better understand options and risks inherent in each.

Listed by class, these financing options include:

- Your own money in one form or another
- Friends, Family and Fools' (FFFs) Financing
- Accelerators
- Loan Financing
- Financial intermediaries
- Equity financing
- Crowd funding
- Asset-based financing
- Mezzanine Financing
- Grants
- Creative operations
- Initial public offerings

We'll spend the next several insights quickly delving into these, some of which you are familiar with, and some you probably have never heard of.

Let's start with funding from your left or right pocket. You may have personal assets with value above any mortgages or loans, or credit cards with credit limits that could permit you to tap into the financing they offer. You rarely need permission to do so, except sometimes from a spouse, but should carefully consider the personal liability attached to these forms of self-finance. Credit card debt is one of the most expensive possible ways to finance your business. Once you are behind in payments, charges from your card company can consume you quickly.

Personal savings certainly rise to the top of the list of methods for financing a new venture. The cost is only the lost interest or earnings of the money invested, and some amount of lost sleep from use of your nest egg in financing a relatively risky venture. But later on, outside investors, or even bank officers, will ask "How much have you invested in this?" And you'll have to face the fact that lenders or investors don't want to be the only ones at financial risk in your venture.

Friends, family members and many unsophisticated investor associates will often invest in you with enthusiasm and few requirements in return. Too many times, optimistic entrepreneurs place too high a value upon their young enterprise, or take money from those who are not legally qualified to invest in your business. We call these companies *dirty investment opportunities* when we professional investors run into these. Cleaning up a dirty company often requires lots of work, even to the extent of offering to refund early investors the money that they gave to the entrepreneur because they were not legally qualified as "accredited investors" to do so. And placing too high a value upon a young business just sets up a roar of disappointment and anger from these early investors when a subsequent, more sophisticated investor reduces the value per share to a more proper amount.

But there are many more ways to finance a young business. So let's continue to explore these.

The "inciting incident:" Movie scripts tell us how and when to look for investment.
By David Steakley

David Steakley, a past President of the Houston Angel Network, is a reformed management consultant. He is an active angel investor, and he manages several angel funds in Texas.

If you are a screenplay writer, you are familiar with the dogma of the inciting incident. In a movie, the inciting incident is the event at the beginning of the story which causes the hero's life to be completely transformed and irrevocably changed, and which makes the whole story unfold. Companies also need an inciting incident, because, more often than not, you often will depend upon selling your story to someone. What is the inciting incident for your company? How can you get to it more quickly and with less capital?

Every good story has an inciting incident. You may not spot it at first. For example, ask yourself: "What is the inciting incident in *The Godfather?*" This one is tricky, because it doesn't occur until 45 minutes into the film, when Vito Corleone is gunned down in the street. This event totally changes the life of Michael Corleone and makes the rest of the story happen. Ok, now you're an expert: quick, what's the inciting incident in *Star Wars?*

The terminology is from the movie industry, but the concept applies to all stories. Every good story has an inciting incident. I am father of four kids, tween to teens, and I sometimes kid them, as a seemingly pointless anecdote trickles to an end, with the capper "...and then you found five dollars?" This is amusing (to me, at least) because it points out that the story lacks an inciting incident.

Story seems to be an artifact of the human brain, and soul. It is a key part of what makes us human. Stories are the most important repository of wisdom, experience, knowledge, and learning. Story telling is often a key aspect of a great leader's talent. For example, while Steve Jobs was abusive, rude, and unappreciative, he had what his colleagues referred to a reality distortion field. He told his team how it was going to be, and even though his story of what was going to happen seemed to be completely unrealistic fantasy, he made his team believe the story, and his teams of believers made it come true.

I found myself explaining all this recently to a company team that was pitching me on its story. The company is building a website to match commercial tenants with commercial landlords. They told me all about why this is such a good idea: hard to manage price discovery in the commercial real estate market; fragmented information about vacancies obtained from landlords and brokers; and the large scale of transactions. They told me about their expertise and their network of contacts, and their early customers, and the promising results so far. They wanted to come to pitch to my angel network.

I told them they lacked an inciting incident. None of the angels in my group is likely to write a check without hearing and believing a story about how something dramatic is about to happen. The very best thing, I told them, would be to come back when the inciting incident has just happened, but the consequences have just begun to unfold. We talked about what this could be: major PR to drive tenants to the site; signing a deal with a major landlord to greatly increase listings; a scheme to source listings at massive scale from public data--there are a lot of possibilities, but they didn't have that element.

When you're selling your company to potential investors, you have to work hard on your story, and the story doesn't really begin until the inciting incident.

Answer: In Star Wars, the inciting incident is Darth Vader's attack on Princess Leia's spaceship.

Can you borrow your way to success?
With help from JJ Richa

J.J. Richa is a successful entrepreneur and technologist giving back to the entrepreneurial community in many ways, including his weekly Internet TV program on entrepreneurism, and participation in several mentoring programs.

There are so many ways to finance a small business. Most of them rely upon some form of debt, often personally guaranteed by the founder(s). So we investigate the most simple of these methods of debt financing first, since most are simple to execute and non-dilutive – that is help you to retain your ownership intact.

Here is a list of common loan types:
- Line of credit – short term working capital
- Term loan –real estate, equipment or other long term capital requirements
- Guarantee based programs:
  - Small Business Administration (SBA)
  - CalCap – California Capital Access Program
  - State loan guarantee
- Economic development programs such as CEDLI

The Small Business Administration (SBA) is a valuable funding resource for many businesses. However, the SBA itself does not actually make loans. Instead, the SBA guarantees bank loans, allowing commercial lenders to make loans that they may not otherwise. The SBA, through its programs, reimburses lenders for a guaranteed portion of the loan (usually up to 85%), making it less risky for them.

In order to be able to obtain a loan, SBA or conventional, you must meet the basic financial institution risk rating, which is known as the "5 Cs of Lending":

1. *Character* – responsibilities and treatment of employees and customers
2. *Cash flow* – debt handling, repayment record, debt liquidity and ratios
3. *Collateral* – hard assets, real estate, capital equipment, accounts receivable
4. – skin in the game, business resources, own risk
5. *Conditions* – economic conditions, market sensitivity ,expense management

Equity financing: great for rapid growth startups

We've spoken of financing a young company through friends and family, known as "inside angels." There are three classes of equity investors for early stage businesses that we have not yet considered. Often grouped into formal organizations, these investors are sophisticated, helpful, and connected.

First, angel investment groups come in all sizes from a few organized angels to large groups of three hundred or more. Each has a process in place to accept applications or recommendations for investment into new companies, and to review these and make decisions based upon their exploration, previous experience in the field, knowledge of the company or industry, or about individual entrepreneurs. Angel groups invest from $250,000 to $1,000,000 or more in qualified investments.

The U.S. Angel Capital Association (ACA) lists over four hundred member groups, located throughout the country. The European Business Angel Network (EBAN), and similar organizations in other countries including Canada, all have web sites with directories of angel groups that are local to you. And even though angel groups syndicate their best deals within their respective associated networks, it is always best to apply to the angel groups nearest your physical location. If you are starting a virtual company with your employees working from home locations, as many startups do, it should be the location of the founder. All angel groups will want to see the founders in person at sometime early in the process. Being located in a distant city greatly reduces the chance of funding success.

With angel groups, you should plan of spending months in the process, from application through funding. You will have to hone your story well, down to fifteen minutes and perhaps fifteen slides in your presentation. Your opportunity becomes real when you are invited to present to the entire group at a lunch or dinner meeting, after which time one of the members or a paid group leader begins to seek commitments from the members to invest in your company. You will be given a "term sheet" during the process, calling out the terms proposed for the investment. These terms have become much more homogenized over the years, with many organizations adopting the same general form and terms offered to new investments. Your principal focus may be on the valuation of the company before the investment is made, which determines the amount of the company you will retain after the investment.

Second, there is a rather new term for those large, individual investors who are usually former entrepreneurs made rich through sale of their previous ventures. These "super angels" act alone or in informal groups, and require that you find your way to them through personal introductions from their trusted associates. The advantage to getting the attention of a super angel is that most operate informally and make quick decisions with little due diligence. This class of investor typically writes checks from $50,000 to $250,000.

The third group, venture capitalists, rarely invests in startups, usually reserving their investments for companies that have star entrepreneurs they have worked with before, or companies brought to them by angel groups or other trusted sources. VCs often invest no less than $2 million in a single deal, finding it difficult to put less money to work and still spend time on boards and coaching entrepreneurs to a successful liquidity event. VCs need much higher exit values to justify their higher amounts of investment, and often want companies they invest in to be worth more than one hundred million dollars at exit, not a riskless task.

The one thing in common with all professional or organized investors is the focus upon the exit, or liquidity event, in which the investors can realize a sale of their interest and a profit from their investments of time and money. For early stage investors, the usual expectation is seven years from investment to expected liquidity. When you take money from any of these sources, you make a pact to build, with their help, a business that can be sold or taken public, hopefully within that time period.

These professional investors look for at least ten times their invested money back upon the liquidity event, knowing that the odds of achieving that are only one in ten, and that half of their investments will probably die before any liquidity event at all. They look for businesses that are in large markets, that can grow fast, and that can achieve revenues in excess of $40 million within five years of founding. Those are difficult goals for most entrepreneurs, making this form of financing unavailable to most, but attractive to those that fit into these criteria.

Is asset-based lending for you?
With help from JJ Richa

The next logical step is to analyze asset-based lending, in which you pledge or assign your short term assets, such as accounts receivable or inventory, to the lender. Often, the lender then tracks the pledged assets until money is received or inventory sold, expecting repayment from the proceeds of sale.

Asset-based financing is a specialized method of providing structured working capital and term loans that are secured by accounts receivable, inventory, machinery, equipment and/or real estate. This type of funding is great for startup companies, refinancing existing loans, and financing for growth, mergers and acquisitions.

One example of asset-based finance would be purchase order financing. This may be attractive to a company that has stretched its credit limits with vendors and has reached its lending capacity at the bank - or a for possibly a startup company without adequate financing. The inability to finance raw materials to fill all orders would leave a company operating under capacity. An asset-based lender finances the purchase of the raw material. The purchase orders are then assigned to the lender. After the orders are filled, payment is made directly to the lender by the customer, and the lender then deducts its cost and fees and remits the balance to the company. The disadvantage of this type of financing, however, is the high interest typically charged.

Handling the reporting for such loans often require some amount of dedicated time. Many lenders require that a transaction report be generated along with a batch of purchase orders or invoices pledged as collateral for the loan. The lender has the right to reject any individual pledged item, and then calculates a percentage of the value as the amount to loan. Ranging from 50% to 80%, you can request an "advance" up to your credit limit, beyond which no more is available, and you must rely entirely upon your own devices to finance further transactions.

Each transaction report also contains a list of money received against pledged items, so that the calculation of available credit remains fresh, and based upon remaining invoices that are not yet overdue. Government invoices are usually not accepted, and any new invoices from accounts that have outstanding invoices more than 60 days overdue are usually also exempted, as are invoices to concentrated customers who account for a significant percentage of the company's business.

Asset-based financing is not cheap. Lenders often tack on charges for management of your account, for a "float" of cash to account for the number of days to clear payments received, and for a periodic audit of the company' accounts. Adding all of these often adds an additional 3-8% to the stated interest rate of the line of credit, sometimes making it one of the more expensive methods of finance.

Finally, some asset-based lenders are "factors" who actually purchase your invoices, hold back a portion of the proceeds to protect against future bad debts, then deduct their fees before remittance and remit a net amount, with the final amount to be remitted upon collection of the money owed by the customer to the factor. Factors redirect your customer's payment to the factor's postal lock box. You never see the cash collected, since the invoice is owned by the factor, no longer by you.

There are many other forms of financing a small business. Let's explore some of them.

Crowdfunding: a roar from a young lion
With help from JJ Richa

Can you imagine having 300 shareholders? With recent legislation and new portals on the Web, it's entirely possible, perhaps for the first time for small businesses.

Simply stated crowd funding or crowdfunding is the raising of capital in small amounts, from a broad base of investors. Usually the investors are non-accredited, and only invest a small amount. It's similar to microfinance, but for the most part using equity instead of a low-interest loan. The object behind crowdfunding is to open up more opportunities for capital to flow into businesses to help them grow and create new jobs. Participants can raise funds without having to do a public offering, which is a costly undertaking.

Crowdfunding is not for everyone. Entrepreneurs who can raise funds in more traditional ways from knowledgeable investors should still lean toward doing just that. But there are many businesses that just won't appeal to professional or knowledgeable investors. Are you an artist with a new record, a new movie idea, a new small product to offer? Perhaps you can attract a large number of investors who just want to support your idea, or get discounts for your product. The returns are not as important to them as the joy of participating in your dream. These are the more likely candidate companies and investors.

In order to participate, certain exemptions and criteria must be met, some of which are:

- No more than $1 million is raised via crowdfunding in any 12 month period; and
- No single investor invests more than a specified amount in the offering:
  - The greater of $2,000 or 5% of the annual income or net worth of the investor, as applicable, if the investor has annual income or net worth of less than $100,000; or
  - 10% of the annual income or net worth of the investor, as applicable, if either the annual income or net worth of the investor is equal to more than $100,000, capped at a maximum of $100,000 invested.
- The offering is conducted through a registered broker or "funding portal"; and
- The issuer complies with certain other requirements. Some of the important ones are:

- o   Public listing of the name, legal status, address, website, directors, officers, 20% stockholders, and more
- o   Share price and methodology for determining the price
- o   A description of the ownership and capital structure of the issuer and a host of disclosures including a disclosure of various risks to investors
- o   Companies looking to raise $100,000 or less via crowdfunding can provide financials that are merely certified as true by the officers of the company. Companies looking to raise between $100,000 and $500,000 must provide "reviewed" financials, which means they have to pay a CPA to check them. Companies looking to raise over $500,000 must provide full-blown audited financial statements, prepared by a CPA. Moreover, every year after a successful crowdfunding offering, issuers must file with the SEC and with investors reports of the results of operations and financial statements of the issuer.
- o   The issuer must clearly disclose any compensation it pays to any person promoting its offerings through a broker or funding portal.
- o   Issuers are not allowed to advertise the terms of the offering, except for notices to direct investors or through the approved intermediary.   Hence, all general solicitations for crowdfunding must at all times flow through an SEC-registered intermediary.

So, what are the advantages of using crowdfunding as your first effort and then going after professional investors? It does prove your business model is attractive to at least some segments of the population, a fact which would be attractive to the later investors. What are the disadvantages? Either too many crowdfunding investors and / or any non-accredited investors in early rounds will most likely cause professional investors to pass and find companies without the complexities in structure caused by crowdfunding rounds earlier.

Accelerators: a recent and positive trend

Often I see executive summaries from entrepreneurs who have never managed any form of business, or even managed employees in their past life, and who don't know the first thing about business formation and managing for growth. I used to tell them to find a partner with knowledge in business creation and management. Although that is still a good idea in many cases, there is a recent alternative available to some entrepreneurs on a competitive basis that seems most attractive and positive.

Accelerators are organizations that selectively accept entrepreneurs into a program of intense coaching in a physical environment sponsored by the accelerator that also provides seed funds for the startup to begin its business.

Accelerators are popping up in college towns, urban cities and near existing technology hubs. Some have become well known in the entrepreneurial community as benchmark operations for others to emulate, including TechStars and Y-Combinator. Others have a more local flavor, catering to single audiences, such as students or graduates of a nearby university.

Another term, *incubator*, is increasingly being used to define real estate operations run by universities or private groups in which the principal added value is the reduced price or free rent and access to resources from the incubator's sponsor. Accelerators, on the other hand, put entrepreneurs through a three week to three month intensive program closely monitored by accelerator management and volunteers, teaching, coaching, aiding and building the fledgling business to make it ready for its next round of financing upon graduation.

And graduation is typically marked by an organized "demo day" in which prominent investors, VCs, angels and super angels are invited to attend and see demonstrations and hear presentations from graduating entrepreneurs. There are many stories of funding deals made on demo day amid the excitement of seeing new, polished startups with great ideas and the beginnings of an infrastructure.

Are you a candidate for an accelerator? You'll give up some small amount of equity to the accelerator, receive some amount of cash in return during the program, and learn more in a short time than you'd expect from more formal education programs.

And don't forget creative fund raising.

Let me tell you the story of how I raised $100,000 to fill a gap needed to purchase a new home for my young family years ago. I had located a beautiful home that would be a stretch to finance, and had arranged for a first mortgage from the bank, and a second from the seller. Home values were rising so fast that I knew I had to move quickly.

So I went to visit a number of customer CEOs, told them my story, and asked them to advance some amount against their future billing from me. In return, I said, I would give them more time than originally contracted for, and certainly would treat the relationship as special from that moment on. Corny? Every one of the CEOs said "yes." And I closed escrow on a home I could not otherwise afford, and which I continue to live in, after its value shot through the roof during the subsequent years.

I sometimes counsel CEOs to consider consulting to their prospective customers or in their industry while they are simultaneously developing their product for market. Consulting fees pay the bills, reduce the stress, and give people confidence in the business.

If you are already purchasing raw materials or services such as development or programming, consider asking your supplier to be a paperless partner, showing confidence in you and your future business by granting you deferred payments. You might be surprised at the positive results, if your needs are real and you treat the relationship well by following through on your promises.

How about offering prepaid licenses to your product or a package of prepaid hours, or a discount for prepayment of purchase? All of these create special relationships with your customers, who show their faith and trust by advancing money to you before receiving products or services. Just remember that you must deliver as promised, and you are eating your meal before its time. You will have later expenses to pay when the revenues have already been received and presumably spent.

Strategic partnerships with suppliers, customers and others sometimes are an attractive way to share the risk and fund an operation. Creating a new company to do this is often a time and money drain, even if it seems easier to do this than to create a relationship within existing organizations.

These are just some of the ways to creatively raise funds without offering equity or taking on new debt. Since some entrepreneurs are completely adverse to sharing equity, and some greatly fear taking on any form of debt, creative fund-raising is certainly worth considering.

Can you finance your company with grants?

I am chairman of a company that, as I write this, is twelve years old and has not yet taken a dollar of outside investment. The company has been funded entirely by grants from the National Institute of Health, amounting to millions of non-dilutive dollars in all. The company has created a product that can be delivered as a service to medical clinicians anywhere in the world, enhancing their ability to understand their patents' problems and needs in less time, using the expertise built into an expert system created by the best minds in many medical specialties.

The company grows in value to its customers and to prospective buyers of the business, but without any dilution of control or ownership for the founders. How refreshing!

In general, grants are made to individuals, companies, businesses, organizations or institutions that are working toward serving the greater good or a greater cause. These grants include funding to educational institutions, researchers, research centers, colleges and universities, or private companies that are researching or developing leading edge solutions in several categories including agriculture, education, energy, health, medical, space, science and technology to name a few.

Grant writing takes skill and immense amounts of time. Often, grants require that you partner with other organizations to deliver the results, or measure the effectiveness of your special project. And often, grants come with detailed accounting and reporting requirements. If you can finance your enterprise through grants rather than equity or debt, you retain control and when it is time to sell your interest in the business, a lower sales price will create a higher return on your personal investment.

There are some grants available even for one person shops, from cities, corporations and even non-profits for just your type of business, especially if you support a social cause, can employ more people, or help turn around a geographic area in need of upgrade.

Both sides must be fair in a term sheet negotiation.
By Basil Peters

Basil Peters is perhaps the best known name in the world of early stage company exits. His groundbreaking book, "Early Exits" has become a textbook for angel groups and entrepreneurs throughout the world. His Strategic Exits Corporation provides M&A advisory services, and he is much in demand as a speaker at angel and entrepreneur events worldwide.

After being an active angel investor for about fifteen years, I realized that many of the discussions I was involved in were virtually identical to ones I'd had many times before. A good example was during the negotiation of a term sheet. These usually involve a handful of angel investors, and a few entrepreneurs, who all want to build the very best term sheet for their exciting nascent enterprise.

Unfortunately, the previous experiences, and depth of knowledge of the individuals are almost always very different. To finalize a term sheet, everyone involved must come to an agreement on some fundamental principles which will have a profound effect on the future of the company. Just a few of these terms include vesting, corporate structure, governance principles, financing strategy, valuation and exit strategy.

Each one of these terms includes aspects of fairness, ethics, law, business, entrepreneurship, psychology and investing. Very often, the initial opinions of the people around the table are radically different. In most cases, these are well-meaning, intelligent people who all sincerely want to find the best solution.

Angel investing today is similar to where venture capital investing was in the mid-1980s. Back then, there was no consensus on best practices in that industry. As an example, twenty five years ago, most VCs used common share deal structures. It was not until the later 1980s that the preferred share structure became popular.

During those times, VCs had lots of conferences where thought leaders gathered to discuss term sheets, deal structures and fund strategies. As a result, there is tight agreement today on the form of VC term sheets and definitive investment agreements. Angel investing is rapidly evolving to the same state of development, as a result of networking, industry associations, and deal sharing between angel groups.

Early stage money: The problem with PPMs
By Bill Payne

Bill Payne *has been actively involved in angel investing since 1980, funding over 50 companies and mentoring over 100 more. He is the recipient of the coveted "Hans Severiens Award from the Angel Capital Association, its highest honor.*

The sale of equity in private companies is regulated by the Securities Act of 1933, which requires that the company either register with the SEC or meet one of several exemptions (Regulation D). A *Private Placement Memorandum (PPM)* is a special business plan defined to meet an SEC exemption. In most cases, those entrepreneurs choosing to raise capital using PPMs retain specialists (many of whom are lawyers) to write their PPMs – a rather expensive undertaking. *I don't fund new companies that have prepared PPMs for investment.* I am an angel investor, that is, an accredited investor who is assumed by the SEC and others to be sufficiently wealthy to afford to lose the investment and supposedly experienced enough to make good choices on fundable companies. Angels, as group of accredited investors funding startup companies, are assumed to meet a Regulation D exemption for purchasing equity in private companies.

Like most angel investors, I have preferences for the terms and conditions of investment and intend to negotiate with entrepreneurs on those terms, such as valuation, company structure, the makeup of the board of directors, liquidation preferences and others. I have yet to read a PPM written for a startup company that meets the parameters we angels generally establish for funding new ventures.

If I don't like the terms offered in the PPM, why don't I insist that the terms be changed to accommodate my partialities as an angel investor? Sounds simple, huh? Unfortunately, upon completion of the PPM, the first thing that entrepreneurs tend to do is sell shares to friends, family, friends of friends and other acquaintances. Then, only after convincing these "unsophisticated" investors to sign up and write their checks, the entrepreneur may approach an angel or group of angels.

The entrepreneur may have already raised half or more of the cash required in this round and is eager to top off the round. The PPM does not meet the investing terms and conditions of the angels. The valuation is too high, or the PPM is written to sell common stock when it really should have been a preferred stock deal, or other critical terms are not present in the PPM. Since many unsophisticated investors have already funded part of the round, it becomes too complicated to renegotiate the terms of the deal.

It is only fair that all capital sources in a given round should invest under the same terms and conditions. There should not be one version of terms for the early set of investors (the PPM terms) and a second version of terms for later investors in the same round. In the long term, different term sheets for investors in the same round leads to unhappy investors. We angels could insist that the entrepreneur go back and renegotiate the terms of the PPM with all the earlier investors, but the earlier investors may or may not agree to the changes. From a long history of angel investing, we have learned it is just easier to pass on PPM deals and move on to the next opportunity. We see many startup investment deals every year – too many for most of us to fund.

Regarding PPMs, my recommendations to entrepreneurs are:

- Don't prepare PPMs to fund startup rounds of investment. It is expensive and may preclude sophisticated investors from funding your deal.
- Pursue smart money, that is, sophisticated investors who will negotiate a fair deal with you and help you grow your company.
- Limit your offering: Only sell shares to accredited investors. In the long run, this usually works best for startup entrepreneurs.

Back to basics: Craft your roadmap. Plan your trip.
By JJ Richa

Business planning is a crucial part of a successful business. Business plans are dynamic instruments used on a regular basis to help owners and executives to plan for future growth, and assess past performances. Included in a business plan are financials, competitive landscape, marketing plans, and projected sales to name a few. Without a business plan, you probably are not sure where you are going, or how you are going to get there, or how you are going to know where you've been. If you don't know these things, how are you going to course-correct if things go differently than forecast?

A business plan:

- Organizes your thoughts to better run your business
- Depicts your roadmap/blueprint, and must be revisited often
- Defines your business vision, objectives and goals
- Determines financial requirements
- Keeps you on track to achieve your goals
- Helps you to be more focused
- Forces you to be more objective
- Determines feasibility
- Serves as management tool
- Assists you in raising capital

I'm not seeking a bank loan or investment. So why make a plan?

A business plan is yours alone. Bankers, financial institutions, and investors hardly look at business plans. But it's a valuable document for you. By creating a plan you are forced to think about your business and how it is structured, the objectives and other critical matters. The plan helps an owner realize how interrelated all aspects of the business are. In addition, it helps you focus your ideas and determine how to best manage your available resources including capital, cash, and people.

After completing your plan, you should be able to answer questions:

- Is there really an opportunity here?
- Can we pull it off?
- Can we make money? Is there potential for profits?
- Where are we?
- How did we get here?
- Where are we going and how will we get there?

Forecasting your finances as part of the plan will help you understand if, and how, you can improve revenue. It's hard to make changes if you don't know where you are, and where you've been.

It helps other answer the following question:

- Will they have a chance to succeed?
- Can they pull it off?
- Will the cash flow?
- Did they make any headway?
- What have they done so far?
- Will they be able to execute and reach their objectives?

As your business grows, a business plan serves as a guide to help you track, monitor and evaluate your progress. Having your short-term and long-term goals written down and in front of you can help keep you on track to reach them. Business plans provide you with the ability to identify risks to your business and what alternatives exist to minimize them. By analyzing your business objectively in the plan, you can address problems before they escalate. Studies found that people who write plans are more likely to put their goals in action and increases your likelihood of success.

Business Plans are not static. As your business changes, your original plan may no longer be as relevant. Review your plan periodically – as often as once per month, but no less than once per quarter – and make updates as needed.

Hugh opportunities do NOT command amazing pre-money valuations.

By Bill Payne

One entrepreneur has a company which appears to be scalable to a $30 million exit value in five to eight years, and a second entrepreneur's venture seems to be scalable to $200 million in exit value in the same time frame. Yet, at the pre-revenue stage of development, angel investors price both companies at a pre-money valuation of $1.5 million.

It doesn't seem right, huh?

But, it is… and here is why. It is possible to grow a company to a valuation of $30 million on one or two angel rounds of investment. But, the working capital and management team necessary to grow a company quickly to sufficient revenues to justify a $200 million valuation will require raising lots more capital. So, the angels who provided the most valuable and risky financing for the gazelle that can grow to a $200 million valuation quickly are going to get diluted by subsequent investors, probably by three to five-fold. They may own 30% after the first round of funding but will probably own less than 10% at exit. So, angels simply must value both ventures at about the same price.

Scalability is a critical factor for angel investment. Because of the risk inherent in funding pre-revenue companies, angels are unlikely to invest in any venture that cannot demonstrate the potential to scale to a $20-30 million in valuation in a reasonable time period (5-8 years).

So, angels won't fund a deal that doesn't scale sufficiently to justify investment, and they tend to value all pre-revenue stage companies at about the same valuation, which is currently about $1.5 million in most parts of the US. Although there may be some variation among business sectors, this is essentially true for software companies, medical device companies, life science ventures, electronics companies and alternate energy deals, regardless of the long term potential.

Back to basics: "What and how" of business plans.
By Bill Payne

Business plans come in several flavors, and you will probably have to create each of them to successfully raise money. Let's spend a few minutes to describe possible forms for your business plan, and more importantly, explain how to avoid common mistakes in using your plans.

Elevator pitch: A two-minute verbal description of your business. Illustrate the problem you are solving and how your solution will delight customers. Imagine you enter an elevator on the twentieth floor and find yourself standing next to an investor. How can you explain your business while the investor is a captive audience?

Video Pitch: A video of your elevator pitch that can be used electronically to introduce your business to investors. Take advantage of the media and enhance your pitch by showing investors a prototype or graphic.

Executive Summary: A one to three page description of your business, summarizing your entire business plan but emphasizing the problems customers are encountering and your solution to these problems. Entrepreneurs usually provide condensed descriptions of the competitive environment, the management team, brief pro-forma financials and the amount of capital required to start and grow the business.

Here are some more tips from Australian entrepreneur, *Jordan Green.*

PowerPoint Presentation: Follow Guy Kawasaki's 10/20/30 rule as described in *The Art of the Start*: Describe your business in 10 slides; deliver the presentation in 20 minutes using few words and large typestyle (using a greater than 30 point font).

Business Plan: A full blown description of your business. Regardless of what you read elsewhere from investors, writing a full plan is a key to understanding all aspects of the business and to creating alignment among the management team, employees, vendors, customers, partners and investors. Some investors continue to demand a full plan and often use these as an outline for their due diligence before investing.

Imagine a fishing analogy: The elevator and video pitches are lures – used to attract investors. After pitching, give those investors a copy of your executive summary. Interested investors will then set up a verbal presentation. Use your PowerPoint presentation to "set the hook." Expect lots of questions from your investor audience. Investors who wish to pursue investment will ask for a copy of your business plan and enter a stage called "due diligence," spending lots of time with you validating the investment opportunity. "Reel the investors in" and close the deal.

Don't spend too much of your time with investors talking about products and technology. Talk about solving customer problems. Why would users select your solution? Be ready to discuss all aspects of your business. Investors fund companies, not products.

Do not hand investors your business plan when you first meet them. They will politely accept it and then likely throw it away before reading. Wait until you have attracted investors and then they ask for a copy of your business plan.

Practice your elevator pitch and your PowerPoint presentation until you can deliver each smoothly. Cover all the materials quickly, leaving extra time for questions from your investor audience. It is usually the interactions during the Q&A period that will cement interest among investors.

Understand the size of your opportunity. Do not estimate revenues as a percentage of the market. Do a bottom's up analysis. Explain which customers will buy how much of your product.

Don't overemphasize the importance of "first to market." Investors know that among successful giants, like Facebook, Google and Internet Explorer, none were first to market.

Be sure to include your contact information in your executive summary and business plan. It is very frustrating for investors to meet an interesting entrepreneur, take a copy of their executive summary home to read, generate more interest by reading it and then discovering you have provided no contact information to facilitate follow-up meetings.

If further along, consider mezzanine financing.
By JJ Richa

Mezzanine is a hybrid of debt and equity financing that is typically used to finance the expansion of more mature, existing companies. Mezzanine financing is basically debt capital that gives the lender the rights to convert to an ownership or equity interest in the company if the loan is not paid back in time and in full. It is generally subordinated to debt provided by senior lenders such as banks and venture capital companies.

Since mezzanine financing is usually provided to the borrower very quickly with little due diligence on the part of the lender and little or no collateral on the part of the borrower, this type of financing is aggressively priced with the lender seeking a return in the 20-30% range.

Mezzanine financing is advantageous because it is most often subordinated to other debt, and treated much like equity on a company's balance sheet and may make it easier to obtain standard bank financing. To attract mezzanine financing, a company usually must demonstrate a track record in the industry with an established reputation and product, a history of profitability and a viable expansion plan for the business.

The rule of Thirds

It is rare when one person starts a company, supplies all the funding, and shares no management tasks or equity with others, and still grows the company to any significant size, worthy of a multi-million dollar opportunity to cash out at exit.

We should think of the creation and growth of a high valued company as the sum of three parts, with three distinct classes of participants helping to make real value out of a raw start-up.

First, there is the *entrepreneur*, the visionary, and force behind the venture from start to finish. The reward for the entrepreneur, after years of effort, time and sacrifice, is measured by what portion of the total pie s/he retains at exit, how much the person continues to participate through that time, and how many other resources are brought in to get to that point. Most importantly, the reward is measured by how much added value the total process creates over time. It is the old story of "100% of nothing is worth far less than 10% of a large number."

Few entrepreneurs can do it alone, with subordinate hired help and no expert management to share the burdens, skill sets and efforts involved in growing the enterprise. So *co-management* is the second group to share in the bounty upon a liquidity event. Often, if not co-founders, this group is rewarded through issuance of stock options from a pool of available options that usually totals 15-20% of the total company's equity divided among all employees. Those who receive options but leave the company before a liquidity event may either purchase those shares represented by the options upon exit from the company, or lose the right to those shares, often 60 days after their exit.

The third group is made of the total number and types of *investors, other than the founder(s).* From friends and family early on, to angels that are not related to the founder(s), to venture capitalists for larger opportunities, these investors have risked their money in the venture for only one reason – to eventually profit from a liquidity event.

It is normal for the first round of organized angels to expect to purchase between twenty and thirty-five percent of the company with their investment. Second rounds, if needed, often drive the founder(s) into a minority position, unless the company has grown significantly by that time and can command a higher pre-money valuation, giving less stock for the same amount of investment. Investments in small companies involve a much greater degree of risk than investment in public companies, which provide immediate liquidity if needed and a ready measure of value at any time. That risk deserves reward if there is a profitable sale or even an initial public offering, rare as that event is.

So remember that there are three slices to the pie to consider when creating your company and again when considering a sale or liquidity event. All three deserve recognition for the risk, time and effort in driving the company to its ultimate value.

Think of it as the *rule of the thirds.*

Find your champion.

If you seek funds from an organized investment group such as an angel fund, venture capital entity, or even an investment club, the first thing you want to do is to find one person to buy into your vision, become excited by your enthusiasm and be willing to become the internal champion for your fund-raising effort.

In some groups, if you cannot find such a person, you cannot even find the way to apply for funding, as some groups make it imperative that any introductions come from the inside, from a member or partner. In others, if you cannot find such a champion after initial presentations to a subset of the entire group, you will not be permitted to move from initial application to the next stages of due diligence and final funding.

And in all cases, simply sending in an executive summary of the business plan via email or filling in an application for funding on a website lowers the chance of success to near nil. If you cannot find someone on the inside, network with accountants, attorneys and bankers to find a name of an influential member or partner.

You may have the most impressive plan in the world, but these organizations see tens of these each week, and often cannot be expected to understand the vision and potential of any at first glance at a document. I receive three hundred unsolicited executive summaries a year, and my investment group, Tech Coast Angeles, sees over one thousand. Together we fund, maybe, twenty-five of these. Although much more than half are disqualified because of geographical location, industry, or amount of money needed, that still is a small percentage of funding to applications.

Banks and lenders often are the same way. Although anyone can walk into a bank and apply for a loan, those who are recommended by a trusted source are treated much more personally and have a greater chance of success.

Spend time finding your champion. Create time to network with members of these groups at their public events. Seek out names from your trusted sources.

Turn the tables: What's an angel look like?

Angel investors, particularly those in organized angel groups, are typically former entrepreneurs who have had successful liquidity events in their pasts, or executives of companies who've retired with the funds from their stock options. Occasionally, an angel is a member of a wealthy family, having little experience managing a business. But most often these angels are skilled at growing companies, calling on their past experience to evaluate and then help entrepreneurs in their early stages of growth.

Several times in our angel group, one of the largest in the United States, we have queried our group as to their motives in being active, risking their money, taking their time to research, perform due diligence and then coach entrepreneurs of young companies. The result of these surveys over time is universally the same. Although most every angel member joins a group to find great investments that will make money for the investor-member, all have other, sometimes more personally important goals. These include giving back to the community in the form of time and investment, or learning about new industries, new advances, and a generation of new ideas. Members want to socialize with those who have similar backgrounds and interests. And members want to participate in the creation of the excitement they universally once felt in the growth and ultimate liquidity event they experienced with their previous company.

Angels come from technology, real estate, medical specialties, and many other industries, bringing a wealth of experience to the table to help evaluate and then coach entrepreneurs.

So how an angel responds to your pitch depends upon his or her background. You should try to find a way to get information about your audience before or even when standing in front of them. What industry specialties do they like, or where did their experience come from? Do you know any people in common? Are they interested in your industry either to be educated or to share their skills and experiences?

Connecting with these people often requires a bit of effort. Networking events are great starting points. Although many of these angels will appear standoffish at the start, if you can find some information from one or more of them before making your pitch, you will be in a far better place to succeed when pitching your idea to an individual or a group.

Don't over-estimate the knowledge of your audience.

When making a presentation to a new audience, the smart thing to do, if there is an opportunity, is to ask your audience by show of hands, if they have some knowledge of your industry or space. If you are making a one-to-one presentation, don't start without a conversation about the other person's knowledge of your space. With that conversation, you create an immediate connection with your audience even before beginning to present, and you know better how much explanation you will need to accompany your most elementary statements. And you will not insult the industry experts by appearing to talk down to them.

When I give a keynote address, I often start by asking my audience, by raise of hands, to tell me how many are angel or VC investors, and how many are entrepreneurs, how many are service providers such as attorneys. Immediately, I can tell how to orient the explanations behind my pre-cast slides, based upon the response. It always works, and the audience should appreciate that the speaker takes the time to orient the talk to the audience, not the other way around.

If your audience is composed of PhD's in organic chemistry, would you want to explain the most elementary teachings in the field? On the other hand, it is most often true that only one or a few of your audience members is knowledgeable in your area of expertise. Address them directly with "I hope you will put up with me as I spend a few moments explaining some of our elementary knowledge to the others." That makes these experts a part of your presentation, able to nod their heads when you do explain these things to the others, instead of looking a bit disdainful that you don't recognize that there are experts in the room.

Don't get hung up on valuation.

I can't tell you how many times I've walked away from deals where the entrepreneur insists on a start-up premoney valuation that is so high, no angel could expect to make a return upon the investment, even with a reasonable sales price for the company down the road.

There is always another attractive deal at the ready, and most have reasonable expectations of valuation. Why fight about valuation, or disappoint the founder at the outset? The real focus should be on smart planning, finding ways to launch and build the business with smart but frugal use of money.

Let me tell you two stories that are linked. The first is of a 2004 startup that I cofounded and led the investment group for several early rounds, then VC rounds. The company has grown to forty employees and a healthy eight figure gross revenue run rate, but has absorbed over $36 million of angel and VC money to do so, and without yet reaching breakeven.

The second story involves the same founder. This one is using outsourced development, support, outsourced customer relations and more. The total capital raise will have been under $600,000 if all goes as planned, and the founder retains majority control of his baby through this and even one optional future round.

For the first, company, the founder's remaining portion is under 4% after all the subsequent rounds, and not yet at breakeven. The second company, with the same founder, finds him with majority control even if the original raise is not enough. For the founder to see any return at all in the first company, the ultimate selling price must be above $40 million. In the second company, better planned, the founder would be made pleasantly wealthy at a selling price of $10 million. The chances of the latter occurring are much greater than the former. This founder was not hung up on valuation for the second company, just upon efficient use of

capital.

Don't be defensive, but defend.

When meeting with investors, during the period devoted to feedback after your presentation, you will hear comments and recommendations that don't resonate with you. Some will be from a misunderstanding of your explanation. Some listeners will challenge your assumptions. Some will seem to ask just plain show-off questions, in which the questioner wants you and others in the room to know that s/he knows more than you do.

You are in a vulnerable position in that room, the salesperson looking for money before individuals who have nothing to lose but risky profits far in the future. You cannot appear to be standoffish, or above responding to some of these inappropriate questions.

Defend your position when appropriate. But listen carefully. Although you may be completely right, the questioner's comment may indicate that you are not getting your points across. That's just as valuable for feedback as hearing a good, new idea.

Sometimes, you will have an opportunity to present to several levels of an investor organization, from first prescreening, to a screening session with many present, to the final meeting of the members or partners. Plan to incorporate the appropriate responses to earlier questions in the presentation to avoid those being repeated. Show that you are both humble and adaptable.

Investment groups including venture capital fund managers will tell you that the very process of defending your plan will help you better think through the rough spots, better launch the business with fewer holes in reasoning, and better connect with resources that can be used to accelerate your growth to breakeven and beyond. The process is always time-consuming and grueling. But approached correctly, the time is well spent and the results almost always positive, even if money doesn't come from the present effort.

Create a ten percent profit model.

Most entrepreneurs, when starting to model their business operations using a spreadsheet, start with expected revenue by month. Then they calculate cost of sales, and then project their expenses, to find the bottom line profit or loss each projected month.

There is a rarely-used twist that makes lots of sense. Add a new row at the bottom of the spreadsheet. Project your revenues and costs as in the original exercise. Then consider that an operating entity should be able to generate a ten percent operating profit based upon revenues, and add a row to your spreadsheet immediately below "operating profit" that calculates 10% profit from sales each month. Compare that with the operating profit as calculated, which surely will be lower, probably negative, for months or even years. The difference is something new – a target for reduction of expenses or addition to revenue for each month in which the calculated number is lower than 10% of revenues.

We are not taught to think this way, but rather to find the month in which we break even in our plan, then calculate the accumulated losses to that point, add all the cash needed for investment in fixed assets, and end up with the amount needed to finance the business to breakeven through equity or debt financing. This new tool gives you that number *plus* the amount needed to make the business a viable entity with a chance of long term survival. The longer the time it takes to break even, the higher the number of dollars needed. Sometimes, the difference is a reminder to consider a reduction of expenses, if revenues cannot be raised from projected levels.

And sometimes, it is just a reminder that we are all in business to make money, not to break even. Just like assuring that your own at-market salary is included in a forecast even if not drawn in cash during the earliest periods, the 10% target reminds us all that the target must be higher than merely breaking even, even if that means reassessing all expenses until the target is met or exceeded.

Outside investors want liquidity not love.

Taking in angel or venture money requires a setting of an entrepreneur's expectations that may come as a shock at least at first. From the moment such an investor looks seriously at your company, the investor or VC partner is thinking of the end game, the ultimate sale of the company or even of an eventual initial public offering. There is no middle ground. Taking money from these sources involves resetting priorities over time. There is no such thing as a lifestyle business with outside investors.

To protect against such an event, almost every professional investor includes a clause in the investment documents which allow the investor to "put" the stock back to the company after five years, requiring the company to pay back the investment plus dividends accrued during the term of the investment. This sword hanging over the company is not often used, but is a constant reminder that an outside investor is serious about getting out, hopefully in less than five years, at a profit, usually from the sale of the company. Many companies find themselves at the five year point completely unprepared for a sale and without the cash resources to carry out such a repurchase of investor stock, making the clause moot.

There are also clauses in many such investor documents that allow the investor to override the founder and force a sale of the company if a proposed sale is attractive to an investor for liquidity, even if the founder feels that there is much more potential if the business is not sold at the present time.

Finally, it is an unfortunate fact that when a company needs money and has not met its original planned targets, the newest investor prices the round at a level below the last or last several rounds of financing, angering and frustrating previous investors who took what they perceive as the greatest risks by investing before the business proved itself. The last money has the first say – in valuation and in sometimes forcing draconian terms that require prior investors to contribute a proportional new investment to retain a semblance of their original rights and avoid dilution or worse yet, involuntary conversion to a lower class of stock. As the years progress with typical VC firms seeing lower returns than expected by their limited partner investors, such terms are more common in secondary rounds of financing, causing a real riff between angel investors and their former close allies, the VCs, with whom they had once coexisted as suppliers of deals at expectedly higher valuations at each stage of investment.

So be aware that professional investors are in your company for the eventual large profits at the liquidity event. They are your friends only as long as you meet or exceed planned growth and value. They tolerate you and your management when the numbers are a bit murky but with an explanation that is believable and correctable. They act in their own best interests when things go south. That's just the facts.

Raise cash from trusted, close resources first.

This insight follows closely the conclusions from the previous declaration, that professional investors negotiate tough terms, from provisions of control over asset acquisition, eventual sale of the company, future investments, forced co-sale when others attempt to sell their shares and more. And yet, in an earlier insight, we spoke of the problems that come when taking unstructured investments from friends and family. So how does the statement above fit into this sandwich of alternatives?

Trusted, close resources include sophisticated relatives, friends and business associates who know how to structure a deal as a win-win for you and for them, while allowing you to retain control over your vision and execution. Their investment should be structured with the help of a good attorney who understands the mutual goal of maximum leverage of funds with minimum interference in your business decisions.

Remember the admonition that investment from such close sources carries an additional burden for you – to protect your investors and their investment as if they were your alter egos, offering money as if from your own pocket. Such money should never be taken without clear understanding of the terms, whether a loan with a reasonable interest rate and strict repayment terms, or an investment valuing the company at an amount considered reasonable by a third party professional, even if as a sanity check as opposed to an appraisal. This money is personal, an investment in you as much or more than in your company. The degree of care you take increases with the reduced distance between you and your investor.

My very first investment as a professional angel was in a small startup where the entrepreneur's vision fueled my imagination in the audio market niche where I had run a business in an earlier life. I was so enthusiastic that I coached the entrepreneur to approach his mother, who invested $50,000 under the same terms as my investment. A small venture firm and a few more angels rounded out the total investment. As the company grew and became profitable, it became more visible to others in the market niche. Two of us who invested served on the board of the company, advising the first-time entrepreneur with our business and industry experience. Several years later, with the approval of the board and entrepreneur, I was able to engage a very well-known potential acquirer of the business who offered an attractive price for the still-young but successful enterprise. After weeks of negotiation, the entrepreneur suddenly disengaged, claiming that he was no longer interested in a sale of his company. The rest of us were shocked and disappointed that after weeks of work and a fair price, we were left with nothing but to follow his lead and disengage. Shortly thereafter, in a board meeting, I brought up the issue of starting to pay board members for service in cash or in stock options, typical for outside board members but rarely for investors. The entrepreneur was angry, abusive, in his negative reaction to even bringing the issue to the board for a discussion. Five years had passed from my original investment in what I now clearly perceived as investment into a lifestyle business, one where the entrepreneur had no interest in selling or sharing. I resigned from the board on the spot and negotiated a sale of my stock to the entrepreneur at five times the earlier investment, a fair return for both, since the company was by then worth much more. It is now years later, and his mother along with other early investors are still in the passive game, not likely to see liquidity from this mistaken investment in an entrepreneur unwilling to take money in exchange for the eventual promise of liquidity.

Why tell this story at all? Mother is surely satisfied as a passive investor who probably would have given her son the money without structure. The other investors are probably in the unhappy never land of not being able to see liquidity after a decade and unable to write off the investment as a loss for tax purposes. This story would probably have ended in a lawsuit if a larger professional investor had been involved, since the entrepreneur did not follow the rules and seems to have no desire to do so.

Trust works both ways. Take money from close resources, but treat it as if the responsibility is even greater to protect the investors and their money than from a professional. These investors trust that you will do the right thing for them if at all able.

Money comes smart or dumb. Find Smart.

This statement could be considered controversial. We have previously made the case that professional investors demand more in the form of restrictive covenants and lower valuations. Now we explore the other side of that coin. Professional investors usually bring "smart money" to the table, defined as money that comes along with good advice and great relationships for corporate growth. Often, that money is worth more than the cash invested, because the investors who often become members of the board, bring a wealth of experience, insight, relationships and deeper pockets to the table.

I serve on the boards of several companies with just such VC talent at the table, partners in firms that made subsequent investments in companies where I either made early investments or led a group of fellow investors in early rounds of finance. Each of these companies needed more cash than professional angel investors were willing or able to provide, and we turned to the venture community for larger investments.

Attracting a VC investment means finding a partner in a VC firm who is willing to champion your opportunity before his partnership and then represent his firm with a seat on the board once the investment is made. In a number of cases, these VC partners have made the difference between success and failure or at least growth vs. stagnation. These VC partners have relationships with later stage investors further up the food chain, with service providers, with potential "C" level senior managers, and with other CEO's with great timely advice or partnering opportunities. In one such recent case, the angels were tapped out at $6 million invested, an amount far above their usual taste, but for a company with a billion dollar potential. The VC's that subsequently invested $18 million to date are looking for the billion dollar valuation someday, well beyond what angel investors usually are able to project from their own resources. Whether this business and entrepreneur make it to the rare billion dollar club or not, without the VC guidance there would have been little opportunity to even dream of such a goal. There is no question that the company took smart money and leveraged it for maximum growth, using the money, guidance, contacts and more from these large VC investors.

Is it the jockey or the horse?

Early stage investors have been arguing over this for years. Do they bet on the entrepreneur (jockey) or the business idea and plan (the horse)? This is serious stuff. If you are looking for money, this question will certainly come up in one form or another when you approach professional or organized angel or VC investors.

My answer always varies as I examine each deal, sometimes deferring and passing on an investment because of an uneasy feeling about the entrepreneur, even if the business plan seems able to capture the market. Speaking for others, I see VC investors jumping into deals knowing that soon they will push to replace the entrepreneur with a professional, experienced manager that the VC has vetted and trusts.

I have bet on the entrepreneurial jockey a number of times and been blind-sided by after-investment behavior that completely reversed my opinion about an entrepreneur's ability to manage growth to breakeven. Other times, the entrepreneur went on to assemble a great team and execute the plan as it inevitably changed again and again.

Although this debate will continue for ages, I tend to fall on the side of betting on the jockey, simply because it has been a rare business plan that did not change again and again seeking a successful model in the marketplace. And great management is able to morph a company to adopt without destroying the culture of the company in the process.

What if you were the investor and someone walked into your office handing you a business plan executive summary that floored you with its brilliance? And what if that person admitted immediately that he or she had no team and was not the person to take this plan to market? Would you, as an investor, plow money into the plan and help to incubate the idea into a real enterprise? I would not, nor would most all of those I co-invest with. There are millions of great plans that failed over the years for want of a great management team. And I am sure there are many, many average plans that developed into great companies with the help of a great team.

So if you are one of the entrepreneurs without experience or ability to take your great plan to market, admit this early and form a team that investors can trust to do this, personally stepping into a position that fits your core skills, be it marketing, sales, development, or other areas required by a young company.

It would be refreshing as an investor to meet an entrepreneur with a great plan and a pre-formed management team fronted by the strongest possible leader, even if the entrepreneur offers to take a back seat in order to make the vision a grand reality.

Be approximately right rather than exactly wrong.

I love this statement from John Tukey, coiner of the word 'bit' to describe a single switch of digital micro-data. Tukey was a statistician, one you would expect to describe events in terms reeking with precision.

Instead, Tukey implored us to think in terms of relevancy, cause and comparisons to known events. And all this ethereal talk makes me think of how we investors and entrepreneurs are often led to search for instances in which our plan can be wrong, based upon a past measure. Or how one fact in an argument can be disproved, making the entire argument in error in the minds of some.

Yet, if we do bet upon the jockey with more weight in our decisions to invest than upon the horse (or business plan), then our goal is to be approximately right and not to discount the plan for failure of one element which can be proved precisely wrong.

I made an investment in 2000 in a company that a decade later returned 110 times our investment at its IPO on the NYSE. I invested in the jockey even though I liked the plan. And that plan changed several times during the early years, molded into one that worked unbelievably well, enough to create an entire debit card industry which the company dominates today. It would have been easy for early investors to find reasons not to invest based upon any number of facts upon which the original plan was based, many of which could be proved exactly wrong in the minds of fellow would-be investors.

Early stage investing is more risky than later stage when we can look back, know and measure prior successes. But the bet is more often upon the jockey and that s/he will be approximately right by maneuvering the plan with the management team, rather than executing a plan that was flawed as originally written, and in retrospect exactly wrong.

Consider all resources before seeking investment.

I cannot tell you how many times I have seen executive summaries of business plans in which the entrepreneur seeks $5,000,000 to build the business.

First, few startups can use that much money today with all of the virtual services available and increasingly inexpensive methods of development, prototyping and marketing. Second, almost no professional investor will consider putting that much into a startup until there is proof of market demand, product viability or some other mitigation of failure.

Third (if you're keeping score), it is not wise to dilute the founder's ownership greatly in the first round of financing. The investors want a motivated entrepreneur, and it is certainly more difficult to motivate a twenty percent owner than a sixty percent owner.

Fourth, there is the matter of control. Entrepreneurs have a vision for what and how to create and build a great business. Giving control over that vision to others early on often dilutes the vision and is a disincentive to the entrepreneur.

Professional investors love to see companies where the first round of financing came from the entrepreneur, showing "skin in the game" and more motivation to succeed because of money invested as well as time and creativity.

There are so many resources for early money to validate an idea, turn it into a product and increase the value of the company before professional investors come into the picture.

Starting with credit card debt or a personal loan and working through money from friends or family, or simply consulting to earn money for investment, entrepreneurs should consider early resources for capital to produce a prototype, do market research or start to build a team. Once there is progress in any of these critical areas, raising professional investment is easier and the likelihood of a higher valuation makes for retention of more equity during the first important professional round.

Address the five risks to increase your valuation.

In the creation of a new enterprise, there are five principal risks to be addressed by the entrepreneur. Professional investors will probe these five risk areas and make the decision to invest based upon comfort with each. So it is important for the entrepreneur to identify, address and mitigate each of these in order to increase valuation and decrease the risk of ultimate loss of the business.

First: Product risk. Is the product or service possible to produce at all, let alone economically enough to compete in the marketplace? One way to mitigate this is by using early money to create a prototype, to perform market research, to complete the first generation of the product, or to deliver the service to a satisfied customer.

Second: Market risk. Are you ahead or behind the market with your product or service? Will the public respond in numbers to buy, license or rent your offering? This risk can be mitigated by finding a customer willing to purchase as soon as a proven model is completed, and willing to state this in writing. Another is to gain the support of a core vendor who is willing to offer special extended terms to the company as its investment in creating the product in a finished state. A third demonstration of overcoming market risk is by holding controlled focus groups and gathering information from unbiased potential customers supporting the acceptance of the product or service.

Third: Management risk. A great idea often fails from the inexperience or inability of management to bring the idea to market. Similarly, great management often can manipulate an original idea or business plan into one much more attuned to the market, adding tremendous value that might have been lost sticking to the original plan.

This is sometimes labeled "execution risk" addressing whether management can create and run the company producing the product acceptable to the marketplace.

Fourth: Financial risk. Any new enterprise is at risk if there are not enough resources to get the company to breakeven, which is a proxy for stability. If a company truly needs five million dollars to get to breakeven, investors that provide the first million are greatly at risk of the company failing to raise the remaining capital or of subsequent investors valuing the company at a lower price than the first investors, causing a "down round" in which the early investors are punished for taking the first risk.

And fifth: Competitive risk. If there are high barriers to entry with such protections as patents, long development time already spent or contracts with the major potential customers, then the risk of a competitor with more resources jumping into the frothy pool and taking advantage of the demand created by the company is minimized.

Reduction or elimination of one or more of these risks increases the valuation of the company and certainly improves its chances of survival and growth.

Personal Guarantees are a fact of life for many entrepreneurs.

Starting and running a small or growing business can be a challenge to the most confident and optimistic entrepreneur. And the process of borrowing money or financing asset purchases can be an eye-opener for those who are not used to today's lender and seller aversion to granting easy credit.

Most any entrepreneur with a clean credit record can obtain a bank card with a $50,000 limit, if s/he is willing to give a personal guarantee and has enough assets to back the promise it contains. As the amounts get higher or as banks get into the picture, the negotiation around a personal guarantee becomes more of an issue with the lender and the entrepreneur. As a rule of thumb, a company with a majority owner in control will be required to provide such a guarantee for most any borrowing of significant size in relation to assets.

But what happens when the entrepreneur has taken investments from one or more outside investors and may not even own a simple majority of the company's stock? To most lenders, the guarantee is still a requirement, putting the entrepreneur in a position of additional risk that is not spread among the shareholders.

At least one company has entered the market providing personal guarantee insurance to bridge this important and uncomfortable gap between risk and comfort. For a fee, insurance can be purchased that will back up most or all of the guarantee in the event of a default, allowing the risk to be mitigated with cash. Since this is a new area for insurance coverage, there is much interest but little experience to create actuarial tables for the insurer or stories to tell for candidate customers. But the very idea is one worth investigating if the problem is one you face.

All entrepreneurs assume risk when starting and growing a business. It is only smart to consider ways to mitigate risks when opportunities to do so arise.

Beware the "dirty cap table."

When you seek professional investors, whether organized angels or venture capitalists, one of the early questions you are asked is "How have you financed the business so far?"   Investors love to see entrepreneurs who have used their own money to ignite their businesses. But often, entrepreneurs turn to others for initial capital. Describing that capital using the phrase "friends, family and fools," or "FFF," has become as common as to be trite. And even more recently, "crowd sourcing" has been enabled by the Internet – seeking many investors at a small amount per investment.

The problem in taking such money rests in the legality of taking money from non-accredited investors, people who do not meet the SEC standard for making non-public company investments. Currently that standard requires a minimum of $200,000 in annual income or over one million in net assets, including the value of the investor's principal residence. Since many small investors in a young business do not meet that standard, there is a chance that the company has taken money that it should not have taken, according to SEC rules. There is an exemption for members of the entrepreneur's family and in some cases for close friends with intimate knowledge of the entrepreneur and of the plan and, of course, for employees of the company. It is worth checking with an attorney to see if such investors are truly exempt.

Some small companies work to create "private placement memorandums," attempting to protect themselves against this problem, couching the proposed investment in legal language stating the risks involved in making the investment. The PPM does nothing to mitigate that problem when the investor is not accredited.

To compound the problem, often stock is issued by the entrepreneur without filing any report of such issuance with the state of issue.

The sum of these problems is that a disaffected investor can sue the entrepreneur or the entrepreneur's company for a rescission of the investment and return of the money invested if the money was taken improperly, especially when the business has failed and the investment lost, putting the entrepreneur at risk for the loss of additional personal assets.

The cure for this, when professional investors enter the picture, is for the company to craft a "rescission offering" to those shareholders who invested illegally, offering to repurchase their shares at full value invested. This is sometimes difficult since it often happens just at the time a company needs new money most and is in the process of seeking that money for growth. If a previous investor does not accept a rescission offer, there is some insulation provided to the company against a future lawsuit by that investor.

So, plan to take money only from qualified investors. Check with your attorney if there is any doubt. The risks of a problem rise with unmet investor expectations, and fade with success. But sometimes, such behavior will cause a subsequent angel or venture capitalist to pass on an otherwise good opportunity, and that would be a shame, one that could have been avoided by diligent process in the early investment cycle.

How Do Investors Value Your Business?

Any small business entrepreneurs expecting to find equity financing from angel or venture capital investors should be aware of the many ways sophisticated investors use to value a candidate business, and should be prepared to supply information to the investor to help in that process.

Financial History and Projections

The importance of accurate current financial statements cannot be overstated for businesses with a track record. If there is no record of revenues, see the "The Berkus Method" at the end of this insight for valuing the business before revenues. An entrepreneur should "know his numbers and be able to defend them" during early meetings with candidate investors. At the least, historical numbers must include the latest income statement and balance sheet, showing activity through the latest period. If the business is not a startup, expect to supply income statements for the past several years as well, to emphasize trends in revenue and costs.

Detailed projections for the next 12 months are a must. Beyond that, projections should be made for two additional years, but need not be in account-by-account detailed format. Sophisticated businesses will also create a cash flow projection for the same period, showing cash used and remaining at the end of each period.

How Much Money Can I Get?

Here is a question with a circular answer. To grow your business to a size that will be attractive to a VC or angel making an investment now, you've got to show that the business will be large enough at the time of the investor's liquidity event (cashing out) to make the investment attractive at all.

Most VC's look for a 10x opportunity – that is – a ten times increase in the valuation from investment to liquidity event. Later stage investors sometimes look for less, since the business has already proven its capability to stay in the game and has already completed its product development cycle, eliminating more risk for the investor.

So you've got to play with the numbers to determine your level of comfort. The more you ask for – the more equity you give up. Completing this exercise often leads an entrepreneur to lower his expectations about the amount of money to be raised. Try this example:

You want to raise $2,000,000 today. Your projections and the analysis we'll undertake below lead to a possible valuation of $40,000,000 in five years, assuming that you meet your plan, and allowing for a 50% discount to the plan numbers during the investor's evaluation. That means – using the 10x expectation for return – making the business worth $2,000,000 today at best. To raise $2,000,000, you must give up 50% of the post-investment equity (the current value of $2,000,000 plus the investment of $2,000,000). The post-investment value would be $4,000,000. When multiplied by 10x, the target valuation at exit would be the $40,000,000 quoted above. It is a fact that very few businesses reach the $40,000,000 valuation hurdle.

Remember that the investor will include the full number of shares reserved for your present or future option plan – usually 15-20% of total equity – making your personal equity 20% less when calculated as "fully diluted," or including a reserve for options. Therefore, in the example above, you would control less than 50% of the company at funding if you received $2,000,000.

Given the strong desire by entrepreneurs to keep controlling interest in the early stages of growth, the amount that can be raised must be lower than $2,000,000 in order to accomplish this goal.

So the circular reasoning exercise returns. Raise the projections (and sell the investor on the increased projections as a result) or lower the amount of capital to be raised in this round. Future rounds should be at higher valuations if you meet your plan, making dilution of your equity less onerous at that time.

With this in mind, let's explore a number of methods to value your business. Many investors use a combination of methods, throwing out those that do not fit the appropriate form of business.

Corporate Valuations Using Various Methods

There are ten recognized ways to value a business. Some are inappropriate for young businesses or those engaged in certain enterprises, such as software development - where fixed assets are not usually important enough to use for purposes of valuation. Here they are, with short explanations of each:

1. Sales Multiple:

The usual limits for use of a sales multiple for valuation are from .5 to 4 times gross revenues for similar businesses. There is some latitude based upon the growth of the Company, using trailing (last 12 months), actual (fiscal year projections) and forecast (next twelve months or next fiscal year). For some businesses, when purchases of goods for resale are a large component of cost, the value is determined after first deducting all cost of goods purchased from third party sources. (A $3,000,000 business engaged in resale of hardware costing $1,700,000 would be valued as if it were a $1,300,000 business for this purpose.)

2. Price Earnings Ratio:

This traditional method of valuation has been applied to companies in all industries, and is the most often quoted method of valuation for public companies. A P/E multiple of between 5 and 30 is common, with growth of company and growth of industry directing the selection of the number. The market sector in which the company works usually has a narrow range of price earnings multiples. You can find that average number in the quarterly *Business Week Magazine* report of public company earnings, among other resources.

Earnings for this, and other valuation methods below, are usually based upon net income after taxes (or reserve for tax), but sometimes are calculated before deducting interest and tax, with the assumption that borrowing is a function of capitalization, not earning power, and tax is a reflection of a company's current status within a multiyear tax planning horizon, perhaps with previous losses shielding present tax liability.

3. Free Cash Flow Model:

This method is often used to value privately held companies with a range of five to eight times the cash available to spend after operating expenses are paid. Free cash flow is important when the buyer intends to finance the purchase using the revenue from the purchased company itself.

4. Book Value Method:

This is the basic net worth of the Company on the balance sheet. It is not relevant for early stage companies, since the value of the intellectual capital and future growth are discounted entirely using this method. This value is often multiplied by two or three times in growth environments, then used as a sanity check against other methods.

5. Liquidation / Salvage Value:

This value is only used as a minimum floor below which no offer should ever fall. It represents the amount the company or a secured lender would realize in a distressed sale, and is never high unless the company owns significant undervalued real estate or fully depreciated working assets.

6. Replacement Value:

This is one of the best ways to create some minimum value, especially for young companies, or where the investment in technology has been heavy and the life span of the technology is long. Replacement value goes up where there is a high barrier to entry due to proprietary tools or patents. The problem with using either liquidation value or replacement value is that usually an appraiser is required to determine the value. The cost for the appraisal is often a barrier to a small company's use of this method.

7. Similar Company Transaction:

A very logical way to examine the value of a company is to base the value upon what someone else is willing to pay for a like company. This is often done with public companies. Unfortunately, using public companies for comparison greatly overstates the value of private enterprises.

Private statistics are rarely available, except when public companies purchase privately held firms and must reveal the amount paid in their 10-Q and 10-K forms for public scrutiny.

8. Recent Same-Company Transaction Price:

This value often sets the basic minimum if there has been such a transaction in a relevant time period. Qualifying transactions would include actual company share sales prices, qualified stock options granted (which are taxable if below market value), valuations by independent appraisers (if used for Employee Stock Option Plans under ERISA or IRS Rule 409a), or internal buy-sell transactions between partners. There is flexibility here, as in any valuation, by the negotiation of how the payment is to be made and over what time period.

9. Internal Rate of Return Method:

Internal rate of return is a classic financial methodology used in valuations, where projected profits are discounted back to the current period. The problem with early stage companies is that most of them do not have a stable enough history to rely upon the numbers. In more stable environments, the calculation might use up to ten years of projected cash flow, discounted back to present value and discounted a further thirty percent for risk. Technology companies would never use more than five years, and would employ a higher discount factor of forty percent or more. Sometimes, the period is reduced to three years for such high risk technology companies. To find the valuation using this method, use your projected net income after tax for each of the next three years. Calculate the present value of each of the two future years by deducting seven percent from year two from the net number and fourteen percent for year three. Multiply each of the three results by 70% as a risk reduction. Add the three resulting numbers, and you have the three year internal rate of return. If the value of your business is so high that it would take ten or more years of cash flow to pay the purchase price for your shares, the company is too highly valued for most investors, unless strategically "buying" technology not cash flow.

10. Comparable Public Company Valuations Method:

One way to find the value of your enterprise is to compare it to similar companies already on the public market. Usually, an investor making such a comparison will deduct about 20% of the value of a comparable public entity in calculating your value, just to account for the intrinsic value of being a public company. This sanity check may surprise you – as many small public companies are now valued at less than their cash reserves, a sign that the market does not expect such a business to be able to become profitable in time to protect its cash on hand. To find the "market capitalization" (enterprise value) of a public business, visit *MSN Money* or *Yahoo Finance* and look for "market capitalization" within the summary of financial information for a listed company.

The actual value of a business is often determined as a blended average of the ten methods above, subjectively placing more or less weight upon one or several of these.

Then there's The Rule Of Thumb Method:

There is an eleventh method – but it is one I use only as a rule of thumb to size up the first ten. For early stage companies, I use the *"Berkus Method"* approach which you will find in the very next insight. This one is used only for businesses in their earliest stage in an attempt to quantify value based upon reduction of risks among other measures.

Valuing an early stage company is not a precise exercise, even if the above methods lead you to believe that there is some precision in doing so. Yet the value of the business is most important to determine at each stage of equity financing to strike a careful and fair balance between the needs of the entrepreneur to retain control at the early stage and of the investor to find opportunity for reward to offset his risk of investment.

The Berkus Method: Valuing an Early Stage Investment.

For those of us who've invested in early stage companies, especially technology startups, we have confronted a universal problem. There are many ways to project the value of a company for purposes of pricing an investment, but all rely upon the revenue and profit projections of the entrepreneur as a starting point. Many formulas then discount those projections according to some set percentage or by assigning weight to elements of the enterprise.

And in my opinion, all fail to take into account the universal truth – that fewer than one in a thousand startups meet or exceed their projected revenues in the periods planned.

Years ago, confronted with the same conundrum, in the middle 1990's I came up with a method of assessing the value of critical elements of a startup without having to analyze the projected financials, except to the extent that the investor believes in the potential of a company to reach over $20 million in revenues by the fifth year of business.

First published widely in the book, *Winning Angels* by Harvard's Amis and Stevenson with my permission in 2001, the method has undergone a number of refinements over the years, particularly in the maximum assigned to each element of enterprise value, reducing those amounts as the investment market adjusted from the craziness of the bubble to more logical values in the years that followed. Because the Internet has such a long memory and documents from the distant past can be found with ease, a search the "The Berkus Method" today will yield a number of conflicting valuations culled from the many subsequent publications of the method over the ensuing years.

Here is the latest fine-tuning of the method. You should be able to adopt it to most any kind of business enterprise, if your aim is to establish an early, most often pre-revenue valuation to a start-up that has potential of reaching over $20 million in revenues within five years:

If Exists:	Add to Company Value up to:

Sound Idea *(basic value, product risk)*	$1/2 million
Prototype *(reducing technology risk)*	$1/2 million
Quality Management Team *(reducing execution risk)*	$1/2 million
Strategic relationships *(reducing market risk and competitive risk)*	$1/2 million
Product Rollout or Sales *(reducing financial or production risk)*	$1/2 million

Note that these numbers are maximums that can be "earned" to form a valuation, allowing for a pre-revenue valuation of up to $2 million (or a post rollout value of up to $2.5 million), but certainly also allowing the investor to put much lower values into each test, resulting in valuations well below that amount.

There is no question that startup valuations must be kept at a low enough amount to allow for the extreme risk taken by the investor and to provide some opportunity for the investment to achieve a ten times increase in value over its life.

Once a company is making revenues for any period of time, this method is no longer applicable, as most everyone will use actual revenues to project value over time.

Think ahead if you will need more money later.

Some businesses just can't fit within the angel capital or friends and family model for raising funds. Sooner or later these businesses will have to seek venture capital and accommodate the needs of the venture community in negotiating the terms of an investment.

First, VC's in general cannot invest in 'S' corporations or limited liability companies (LLC's). This is only a minor problem in that both forms can convert easily into 'C' corporations at low cost and little consequence.

More importantly, VC's will worry over a number of issues when looking at a company and deciding about an investment. Is the price paid for shares by previous investors excessive, creating a post-money valuation too high for the actual value of the company? If so, the VC will contemplate a "down round" - that is: offering an investment where previous investors find their investments instantly worth less than their original value, even if the investments were made at high risk and years earlier. No one wants to face this, but the need for money and the possible overpricing of the first rounds may have created an unsustainable valuation.

Second, it is important in the first investment round to face the issues that may be required later by subsequent, more sophisticated, investors such as VC's. These include "tag along rights" which allow investors to sell some shares when others, such as management or founders, sell any shares. Also included are "drag-along rights" in which minority shareholders may be forced to obey the vote of the majority in such important votes as to sell the company or take a round of financing at lower share prices.

Most VC's today are becoming enlightened (as are organized angels), correctly forcing many decisions that might have been dictated by investment documents instead to the corporate board to decide. This allows for a discussion - and perhaps a negotiation - between inside and outside board members in such instances, all for the good of the corporation, not just one class of shareholder. You may recall that board members have a "duty of loyalty" to the corporation, not to their constituent investors. This enlightened thinking reinforces that duty, even sometimes at the expense of profit to the VC's.

How much information do you give to investors?

There is a natural fear of giving too much information to investors after the initial investment is received. CEO's worry that investors will not keep the information confidential and that financial data will find its way into competitors' hands. Others worry that investors will latch onto individual line items within financial data and engage in inquisitions regarding telephone bills, marketing costs and other tactical line items in detailed financial statements.

First, let's cover the absolute minimum legal requirement a company has to provide to its investors. There must be an annual meeting of the shareholders, and that meeting must be announced with a written notice at least twenty days prior to the meeting. (There is a provision that a waiver of notice may be signed preventing this need, but it requires that all shareholders sign).

At the annual meeting (which can be attended by phone), there are actions that require a vote of the shares present either by proxy or in person. These include election or re-election of board members if required by the bylaws of the corporation, approval of any increases to stock option plans (which would dilute the worth of shares outstanding), and approve any additions to the capital stock authorized to be issued. Shareholders may vote on other issues during the year by written consent, including acquisitions, stock issuances, changes to the articles of incorporation and bylaws, and more.

But the question that is most often asked is: "How much financial information must be divulged?" The answer is that the minimum requirement is to provide an income statement and balance sheet to all shareholders annually. There is no requirement that either be detailed by general ledger account, and those statements should rarely be that detailed anyway.   Summarizing income statements with a line for revenues, cost of revenue, general and administrative expenses, sales and other direct costs - all leading to net income, would satisfy the legal requirement for statement of income and expense.

When a company accepts an investment from professional or organized investment groups - such as angel groups, venture capitalists or corporations, there is usually a document signed called an "investors rights agreement" that calls out additional financial and narrative reporting requirements due to that class of shareholder.   These could include the need for audited financials, monthly financial and narrative reporting and more.   That burden is an ongoing cost of taking the investment, much as a public company takes on the additional burden of governmental reporting, both adding to costs over time.

Good relations with investors can be maintained only by keeping current with information between the company and the investors. If there is a concern over some investors gaining a competitive advantage, the amount of information may be reduced to the minimum for some classes of investors.   A good example of this is the information provided to common stock holders, many of whom may be former employees who have exercised stock options and moved on to join the ranks of the competition.

Of course, a public company is not entitled to pare its information to reduce exposure to competitors.   That is one of the many costs of becoming a public entity as many CEO's have found and dealt with over the years.

Be careful how you define your competition.

Professional investors laugh when they hear an entrepreneur state, "We have no competition."   That statement has killed more investment deals than almost any other.   It is a failed litmus test for the entrepreneur, even if the plan is for a totally new device or service that could take the world by storm. Well, come to think of it, this is especially true in such an instance.

The statement shows a lack of research or previous thinking that is a red flag for investors. Whether the entrepreneur has not been able to find companies doing "something like" the plan, or s/he has not considered the most obvious killer of new ideas – doing nothing, it is a faux pas that should never be allowed to happen.

Doing nothing is the main competitor for most products and services, whether a compelling new idea or a seasoned product long proven to be effective. Remember that the buyer must commit resources, money and time, toward the purchase of your product, and even if the product repays its investment in a few months, there may be issues you know nothing about that make no decision the right decision for this and perhaps many buyers.

Consider the state of the economy. Perhaps buyers cannot obtain attractive financing in the current market. Maybe there is advance knowledge of new technologies around the corner that makes any decision today a risky one. It could be that a larger competitor has met with its customers, promising to extend its product line into this very niche. There are thousands of variants of the theme, where no decision is the right decision.

So, do your homework especially well by putting yourself into the minds of your potential customers. Widen your search to include companies with products peripheral to yours, where extension of their product would seem logical, especially if you plan to be successful early in making sales into their market. If you are raising funds, list "do nothing" as a viable competitor in your slide deck. If you are training your sales staff, work especially hard on responding to emotional and factual counters to a final close of a sale. Practice overcoming the potential objection long before standing in front of investors, customers or even your board. After all, fooling yourself should never be an option.

The last money has the first say.

This important variation on "money talks" is an important consideration for entrepreneurs when seeking an investment from professionals such as VC's. Something like a marriage (and often lasting just as long statistically), your investment partner can be a great cheerleader, coach and resource. But the moment things turn sour, including missed plans, some investors on company boards go into a predictable mode of dictating terms for emergency loans or additional investment.

These include forcing early investors to "pay to play," or invest their pre-rata amounts to keep their original percentages, or suffer the consequences of being diluted to the extreme and losing preferences in a liquidation.

The reaction to bad news by VC's controlling the board by virtue of their power to supply additional money, often includes the threat - or reality - of starting the process to find a replacement CEO. So the combination of bad news and VC or professional investors on the Board can be volatile for the founders or management. Angel investors tend to be much more understanding, and usually resort to coaching rather than replacing the CEO during bad times.

These are only a few of the considerations that have caused an increasing number of early stage entrepreneurs to draw business plans for companies that can be grown with angel and friends-family capital. It avoids the increased risks and pressure that come with subsequent VC investments.

On the other hand, if a business needs large amounts of capital in order to succeed, the entrepreneur and board should contemplate the advantages gained against the increased risks, making a conscious decision to go for the growth with such funds or to grow organically – or to grow with a smaller round from internal investors.

About the author...

Dave Berkus has a proven track record in operations, venture investing and corporate board service, both public and private. As an entrepreneur, he has formed, managed and sold successful businesses in the entertainment and software arenas. As a private equity investor, he has obtained healthy returns from liquidity events in over a dozen investments in early-stage ventures. As a corporate mentor and director, he was named *"Director of the Year"* for his directorship efforts with over 40 companies in the past decade.

Dave was the founder of **Computerized Lodging Systems Inc.**, *(CLS),* which he guided as founder and CEO for over a decade that included two consecutive years on the *Inc.500* list of America's fastest growing companies, expansion to six foreign subsidiaries and twenty-nine foreign distributors, while capturing 16% of the world market for his enterprise products. Known as a hospitality industry visionary with many "firsts" to his credit and for his accomplishments in advancing technology in the hospitality industry, in 1998 he was inducted into the **Hospitality (HFTP)** **"International Hall of Fame,"** one of only thirty so honored worldwide over the years.

He has made over 100 investments in early stage ventures, for which he has an IRR of 97%, which includes capital contributions to his two funds (**Berkus Technology Ventures, LLC** and **Kodiak Ventures, L.P.**, for which he is the managing partner). He is also Chairman Emeritus of the Tech Coast Angels, one of the largest angel networks in the United States.

In recognition for adding significant shareholder value for emerging technology companies over the past decade, he was named **"Director of the Year-Early Stage Businesses"** by the *Forum for Corporate Directors* of Orange County, California and **"Technology Leader of the Year"** by the Los Angeles County Board of Supervisors. Dave currently sits on ten corporate boards and four non-profit boards.

Dave is also a senior partner in the twenty year old consulting firm of *Hospitality Automation Consultants, LTD (HACL)*, and lends his considerable visionary and strategic talents to worldwide hospitality chains and groups. He is the partner responsible for business process reorganization, strategic planning, software development and wide-area network infrastructure, and enterprise management systems.

A graduate of Occidental College, Dave currently serves as a Trustee of the College. Aside from this book, he is author of fourteen other books, twelve in the **BERKONOMICS** series, *"Extending the Runway"* originally published by Aspatore Press (and now by the BERKUS Press), and co-author of *"Better than Money!"* All are books for emerging growth technology company executives. Dave serves as Board Member of the San Gabriel Valley Council of *Boy Scouts of America*, former Board Member of the *Forum for Corporate Directors*, and is Chairman of the Advisory Board of the technology arm of the *ABL Organization*, a networking organization of CEOs in high tech businesses.

He is often engaged as keynote speaker for events worldwide, speaking on trends in technology and of legal and practical issues of governance for emerging company corporate boards. He tells stories of entrepreneurs who have wildly succeeded or failed, deriving lessons from each for his audience. His TEDx talk, *"Smile at success; Laugh at failure,"* is available on YouTube as are other of segments of his keynotes. His televised *"Berkus Report"* segment of *Eye on Business*, can be found on Time Warner cable and other cable channels nationwide.

To contact Mr. Berkus for speaking engagements or workshops, email dberkus@berkus.com , or phone (626)355-5375. Dave's books are available for purchase from the above website, or the same source from which this book was purchased.

Subscribe to the free weekly email or blog, www.Berkonomics.com, containing much of the information from Dave's books with lots of comments from readers with their own stories to tell.

Follow Dave on Twitter (@daveberkus) and Facebook (Dave.Berkus).

Other books by Dave Berkus available directly from *www.berkus.com* **or from your favorite bookseller or online store:**

EXTENDING THE RUNWAY
Aspatore Press / Thompson West Publications

The five tools board members and executives can use to help their companies succeed.   How boards and CEOs should relate to each other for growing the enterprise. Fifty-eight critical questions boards and management should consider in order to assure their mutual alignment.

BASIC BERKONOMICS
Hard cover, soft cover and eBook editions

Volume one of this series. Over one hundred critical insights for entrepreneurs, CEOs and board members covering the life of the company from ignition through liquidity event.   Written with basic explanations for terms and methods, as well as insights into planning and measurement for success with small business startups.

BERKONOMICS
Hard cover, soft cover and eBook editions

Volume two of this series. One hundred and one critical insights for entrepreneurs, CEOs and board members covering the life of the company from ignition through liquidity event.   Dave tells over fifty stories to illustrate his insights, culled from his experience as entrepreneur and service on over forty corporate and ten non-profit boards.

BERKONOMICS WORKBOOK

Companion to BERKONOMICS, this very personal journal contains 101 exercises for the CEO or manager that make each of the insights contained in BERKONOMICS come to life in the form of provocative and actionable questions to be answered right on the pages of the workbook. Once completed, this workbook becomes the manager's personal blueprint for business growth.

ADVANCED BERKONOMICS

Hard cover, soft cover and eBook editions

Volume two of this series. One hundred and one critical insights for entrepreneurs, CEOs and board members covering the life of the company from ignition through liquidity event. More advanced insights into planning and measurement for success with small business startups.

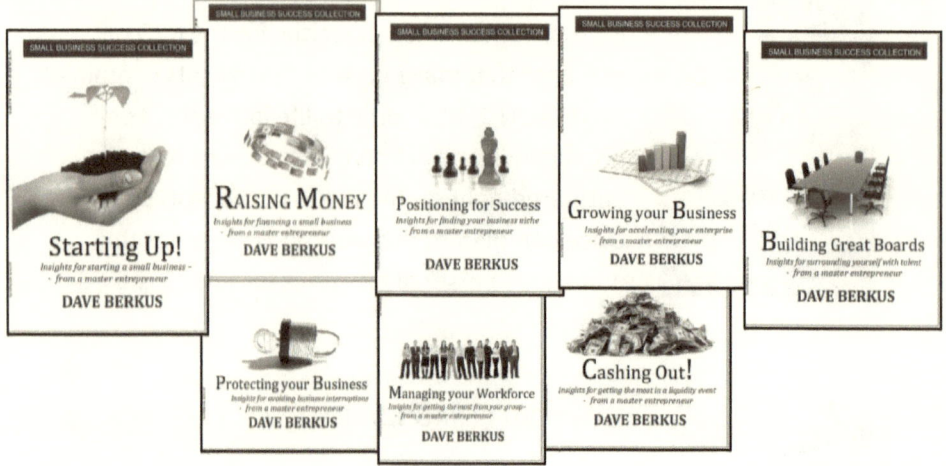

SMALL BUSINESS SUCCESS SERIES
A Series of eight short and inexpensive books or eBooks

Take all the great material in the BERKONOMICS series and slice it by subject, and you'll have these eight inexpensive, short books about issues that you and your management team needs to focus upon today. Ideal for giving to your entire management group for group discussions and business planning sessions.

BOOKS and eBOOKS IN THIS SERIES:

1. Starting up!
2. Raising Money
3. Positioning for Success
4. Managing your Workforce
5. Protecting your Business
6. Growing your Business
7. Building Great Boards
8. Cashing Out!